# Human Wilderness

*poems by*

# Amanda Passmore-Ott

*Finishing Line Press*
Georgetown, Kentucky

# Human Wilderness

## ACKNOWLEDGMENTS

"A Winter Migration." *Tiny Seed Literary Journal*
"In a Canoe on a Lake in Ontario." *Blueline: A literary Magazine Dedicated
to the Spirit of the Adirondacks*
"Wake".*Albatross*
"To Whom I have been Pilgrim..*Wavelength*
"Tell.. *Calliope: A Journal of Women's Literature and Art*

Publisher: Leah Huete de Maines
Editor: Christen Kincaid
Cover Art:Amanda Passmore-Ott
Author Photo: Amanda Passmore-Ott
Cover Design: Elizabeth Maines McCleavy

Order online: www.finishinglinepress.com
also available on amazon.com

Author inquiries and mail orders:
Finishing Line Press
PO Box 1626
Georgetown, Kentucky 40324
USA

# Contents

*We are all filled with a longing for the wild. There are few culturally sanctioned antidotes for this yearning. We were taught to feel shame for such a desire. We grew our hair long and used it to hide our feelings. But the shadow of Wild Woman still lurks behind us during our days and in our nights. No matter where we are, the shadow that trots behind us is definitely four-footed.*

~Clarissa Pinkola Estes
from *Women Who Run with the Wolves*

## A Winged Crossing

I will consider this husk
of cicada, skeletal legs pinned
to the trunk in spruce sap.  I
will become that frame, outline
where body pressed its salty self
out of flesh.

I will attempt beauty
because I'm supposed to be able
to do this and I won't settle
for anything less. I shed myself
over and over, remaining
thinner than bone.

I will let the husk of cicada
be a husk of cicada.
What is it you see? What lingers,
molting where skin casts off—
If there is beauty it is in not knowing.
A winged crossing of this field: cocoons

bobbing on the ends of wheat
or sweat peas, edge where
shells tether themselves like a scent
smoking from burn barrels,
lingering before losing themselves
against the sky.

## Tell

Smell lilac bushes, tumbled rock
beginning to lichen where moss gathers
along the run-off stream.  It is with this
a girl: muddy clay spiraled
on bare arms, down the length of nose
breaking for the mouth before dropping off
the chin, looking at herself wavering
in a shallow pool of rain collected
from the mountain as if she were made of
dirt, as if skin were inconceivable.
I am with her now, just under the low
branches of Hemlocks, swarming in on her
like a cloud of gnats gathered near her face.
I want to see what it is she sees, that
particular mask of my childhood, eyes
the color of river silt beneath
the water: she wore a red skin
of summer doe, skin clay dug
from the bank, pliable thought caught
in dreaming.  It is always like this—we
dream of what goes unremembered
and lose it again when we wake, wrap
them around peripheries of our lives, wear
them like talismans—lilacs dampening air
like humidity.  She washes red trickles
of tributaries down her neck, send
a splattering from her hands across
stream.  Her ear is poised to a name
echoing between the ridges, no more
than wind tunneling down hollow, a distant
answer from a Phoebe.  Away from
the shadow of Hemlock, lavender
blooms along the bank dim to dusk.
I try to follow her, tell her she's lost
a piece of herself, that it fell under
slate rock balancing against the bank—
a lilac blossom folding to the ascending night.

## Human Wilderness

A low brush note of *whippoorwill*
passes beyond whatever closes
our doors to coming night.
Rusting carburetors press weeds
beside bedding deer.  At my feet,
what's left of a snake's discarded skin
is the story of our lives—
no one waits forever.

**Wake**

Clouds leak into lavender
of half dawn where, like beetles
stuck in sap we wait for
the hardness of amber.
It was never supposed to be like this:
silence of the first bird waking,
but we can imagine it
where the flesh goes—
an earth that seemed so solid
groaning beneath it all before giving over
to human voices on the radio.
Some mornings it gets harder to wake
into an awareness whispering *wake up,*
*you are dreaming, you must wake up*—then
wings scudding on air, slight hollow
bones splintering on the ground, no memory
of their marrow, and waking
towards the wall where we swear
there had been a door.

## Severe Weather Warning

Thunderheads stack above
Blue Knob where windmills
catch the updraft—how often
we need a manifestation
to see the invisible. Only
last night bats un-tucked
from the chimney, flickered
across the indigo horizon
to disappear against the stars.
How much wind must feel
under wings of steel
and bone. Deep in the gut
of clouds light gathers.
I wait, drowning
in my own breath.

## Grief is a Haunting

Grief is a haunting of
mid-June wilting to high summer
and the endless rounds
of dead-heading Irises
and placing Dixie-cups half-filled
with beer to keep slugs at bay.
Clouds break their swollen tongues
against the ridge. Specks of graphite
fall where I might capture
a curve of lip meeting a laugh line,
imagined pressure of your fingers
balanced like kindling on his shoulder.
How many times I've watched
the rewind of finch propelled by
some ghost against the downburst,
the mumbled grace of leaf-shiver
an only watchword; and after
air so thick you could drown
in the visible breath of fog gathered
under hanging baskets and tangled
cages of blackberry, a taste
so tart it stings.

## Resting in a Stand of Pine

My body waits for morning's alarm
as trees wait for the sun to shred
last night's fog-slide off Locke Mountain.

Tilled earth musks the way humidity
sinks below skin: my grandfather's hands
pushing onions into index-depth holes
as my girl's thumb digs them out in

up, down our piston dance row after row.

Under this canopy, a bed of needles tells
a different story.  Memories hibernate
in pinecones until fire cracks them open.
One seed in a cluster of seeds: photos

preserved in Ziplocs, a child's cut-outs of
pressed fiddleheads and primrose
curling towards what-if and in the fall
we become mulch pillows for the wandering.

## Become

I dream and un-dream it. A rise where
fences hide an illusion of wild
near bottoms of high grasses. Horses
throwing nervousness, my girl's body
pressed in mud wanting to become
a mahogany or chestnut.
And if when Saturdays came I would
circle the ring at Lakeview secretly
giving the old mare her head and imagine
myself a tautness of muscle beneath
clenched thighs rising towards her gallop.
That time is not here
and I am the disquieted scent
moving in and not a wild thing.

## A Scrapbook of Wildflowers

We are pressing them flat: petals,
stems, compressed memories
preserved translucent sheets
parching like antiqued cut-outs.
Violets turn towards
cornhusks, Indian pipes become
nothing more than outlines.
And there, next to the stinging horse
nettle is a mahogany circle of dried
blood.  It could be mine.  But today
is not about significance, but longing
for milkweed, a decided non-
wildflower whose casing would crack
if pressed, sealed and imperceptible,
your face bent to planting in morning.
*Weed is just a word for wildflower*
*growing where it is not wanted;*
*flower is reserved for something more*
*conspicuous:* your words written
under a pressed lady's slipper still
a pale green, the severed stems snipped
just above the root.
In the garden of our bodies
how do we order the genus
of what is wild? is weed? flower?
I am a longing for milkweeds—
un-mowed hay arching against
Yeager's barn, sun finding our shadows
on the red ply wood—silk threads
unraveled by the wind.  I
only wanted to brush my lips
over them, but we crouched near clover,
sealed our mouths, chewed until no trace
of petal or sweetness remained.

## Barn Swallow

The neighbor girl pirouetting
toe to knee falters in each
new acceleration,
nothing so easy as flying.
I am not so confident
in the spiral she draws
around her center,
or the uncertainty of
a human hand,
how it names nothing
and everything left to say.
Perhaps it is not worth the danger,
brushing off our home's overhang
where gutters grow heavy
in the snow-hush,
and I, deafening in the unspoken
language of things:
a barn swallow's sudden glide
from limb to pole building
a vanishing sentence.

## Flood of '96

We try to forget how
we must invent language
among these broken reeds
when memory of a footless shoe
is all that remains of those two boys.
How the river carved a narrow
asphalt knife across the road—
we balance by not balancing.
How could they know
the river takes less
than four seconds to steal breath?
They didn't hear the irretrievable word
of fence giving way.

## Fledglings

An osprey shadows our birdfeeder
as orange halves arranged for orioles
seep juices like fading suns and finches
poke thistle seeds from pantyhose,
plant them in mouths yawned
and waiting for maybe not tomorrow
or even the next day.

## Flicker

In the early hours a flicker
greets our yard with slender beak
and ruby shoulders, speckled

wings folded snugly to its body,
barely a shadow in the fog.
In my mind another haze lingers—

some remnants of memory
awakened in sleep.  Inside,
plots unravel as the earth

un-tethers the fog, scatters it
in the heat of the sun. Still,
whorls linger at the base

of forsythia bushes. Perhaps
they, too, only want to hold
the night a little closer.

## Cookie Tin of Curiosities

Mixed medium textures
a chalking history of antler and bone.
Bending over, our knees braced on
twigs and variegated acorn shells,
we dust skeletal fragments
with a maple leaf.

Stars, you whispered from bed,
were spirits of all things not
human.  I wanted to hold
what I couldn't have—opening
an old jar to the moon, see
if it would glow under the blanket
after Dusty died—wondering
which twinkle he was running
forever down all that blackness
praying cats could see
in that dark.

In dreams I collect
bones, piecing them
into a cookie tin, waking
to something going smelly
down road, some little history
shuttling out to the sky.

## Harvest Moon

Screech owls warble
as wood smoke columns slice
the moon, a sepia stain over
a photo corroded with dried rings
of some long-gone glass.
Leaves of turning maple linger
where deer eat the last
of September's acorns, their antlers
calligraphy against the sky.
Tomorrow, I'll pull Cala bulbs
from still damp soil, splitting
tubers into pots stored until June
on some dusty basement shelf
next to albums of childhood
Polaroids. Come Spring,
those bulbs will be mush
mixed into the compost heap
where toads sleep the deep sleep.

## Burn

Refractions of ochre, cardamom, burnt
sienna, and mustard seed reflect
off Glendale Lake—an impressionist
painting of the tree line evokes
soft line strokes, dabs of Matisse.
Ripples band the shoreline
where pebbles catch an occasional
leaf or dying lily pad.

Some say these colors are nothing
but dying things, no beauty
resides in flora fading away,
and the season is nothing
if not lingering death. And, yet,
here I find beauty beyond
gardens and flowerbeds overflowing
in dog days of summer. Here,
in lingering death, I burn in leaves
like the first spark of brushfire.

**Kayaking "Little J"**

Line spirals out, catches currents
eddied between boulders, glimpse of
brushed steel where hemlocks balance.
Hiss of reel and trout splinter
our reflection.   One lollygagger
shifts into clouded river rock.

Always here, however brief
I feel as driftwood—
journey of leaf, forgotten lures,
cigarette butts, a sucker barbed by its gills
rounding the bend with water skippers
where blue herons wait.

## All Things Hunker Down

Three juvenile bald eagles balance
inches from the ledge
of thin ice. Beaks part as if
waiting for sustenance
long moved on as seagulls
squawk in whorls overhead.
I catch myself,
a tautness of Adam's apple against
nature's indifference.
This damn sentimentality
creeps up gullet and nothing to swallow
it down. Our feet trek paths
on banks of bloated rivers, always seeking a
glimpse of white feathers beyond
bare branches. We ask ourselves if it is time
to turn back but keep following blue blazes
deeper and higher up trail.
Loneliness, they say, is addictive.
We hold breath with the forest, keep watch
as the blizzard angles across Raystown Lake.
A squirrel leaps from branch
to branch, vanishes on the north face
of birch. All things hunker down
and we too, retrace our steps as snowmelt
wrenches our bones, an exquisite pain
we seek out winter after winter.

## Outside Old Canoe Creek Quarry Mines

No stone is so cold
no stone remembers
so much gone as the sea once
covering it.

Bats' wings deep in the sweep
of flashlight. I envision myself
making snow angels, barely
a child, snowflakes

a hushed ash-fall in a sudden
eruption of porch light.
My mother's face pulls back the blind.
I, a snowshoe hare invisible

for a moment, just one breath.

Today she prepares for white hours
of winter, covering the last perennial
roots with sheets while I try to find
faith in lights strung across valley

like ice-encrusted fireflies
listening for the song or voice
she hears. An absence
something like half my life.

## A Winter Migration

The pine siskins have come south
and evening grosbeaks east.
I wait for an appearance at our feeders
as I have waited for tundra swans
near the river where the monks
of St. Bernadine's keep their silent hours.
In the deep snowy conifers
there is also silence where, if the birds sang,
it would sound as a choir.
Sometimes I feel as if I have been waiting
all my life for the shadow of a white wing
to glide above in night migration,
or the glimpse of yellow feathers fleeting
as an afterimage of the sun behind closed lids.
And sometimes we wait for all those things
others have heard and we have never seen.
I'd become stone myself in the cracks between
logs, peeking up at a sky full of wings.
And, for a while, it would work.
I would forget myself, my own voice buried
like some small animal asleep under the snow.
I thought solitude a place until it disappeared.
But I don't mean to make this about me,
but the birds, between and beneath them,
where silence and syllables collide.

## Cardinal

*for Jack Myers*

I tuck my head under
my arms, press my ear tightly
against the deck rail and listen
to the magnified breath of heart.

Below, a sliver of our creek
at the headwaters, flash
of trout when the sun finds it.

Some evenings hold on
as if they are afraid to die.
Dying is not my fear, but
I think that runoff ditch
has more depth to its vision
than I do.

The occasional song of some
bird, maybe a
cardinal—
the only color that stands
out like a sentient flame
among the bare limbs
of trees.  Perhaps

his song is the monotonous
beat of a tiny heart.

Out there,
so little in the world,
the sound must be so loud—
the only sound he hears.

## Conjure

Beginnings are elusive, caught
in the stagnant backwater eddies
where foam spirals a blanket over
tadpoles and peeps, where a girl skips
the edges of a late April field,
nylon bridle trailing in mud—a whinny
not far distant beyond the springhead.
She pulls out a dog-eared book
as a barn owl's silent arc cuts the loft
door, one more shadow on the periphery.
Mud molds her back as she watches
clouds fly impossibly fast above the summit,
looks to the far rise where fences
disappear into a mirage of wilderness.
She gets up, follows hoof beats echoing
into silence, doesn't look back
through the line of saplings, see
tractor blades furrowing row after row
over the mud-mold of a small child's shadow,
a fossil there at the foot of Brush Mountain.

## Everything is on its Way Somewhere

First, we separate irises
till roots, spread the compost
spiced with cat's mint.
Metronome of your needle
dipping down and out, we
rocked on the off beat
of horse's tails switching deer flies
as our ancestors flint a brush fire
in the sky and I'm afraid for
what lay between that distance.

## To Whom I have been Pilgrim

Afternoon sun filters hemlocks,
condensed just at the bough fanning
weathered green circles between trunks—just
as it did when we were kids catching light
in long strands of fake pearls, aiming
it back to sky in hope of calling
something down, or to bring ourselves up;
either way, we captured something wild
the way a deer's eyes are pulled into headlights
or Luna moths throw themselves into flame.
We saw a huge buck, antlers narrow velvet
peeling off one tine leaning burnished
copper onto its poised neck, eyes locked
somewhere over our crouching heads.
We thought that it was white, something sacred
pinky-swore not to say anything. But our eyes
jumped across flaming marshmallows
blistering on sticks. A barred owl wakes
*who cooks for you? who cooks for you too?*
Lake fog drifts up-glen on scent of crab apple,
deer grunting low beyond rushes and cattails
reminding me how easy it is to confuse becoming
whole with becoming someone else.

## Canoe on a Lake in Ontario

Green meteors dropped off horizon.
I felt a thousand years old.
I felt it would be a good time to die.
All night I tried to grab stars from water,
bring them into the canoe to roll
among an iridescence of salted minnows.
I passed through to elbow
breaking up the Milky Way.
A loon surfaced near shore.
I wondered if she found
something I could not, a closeness
of bone where wings would be if I could
sift even one star from the water

## Lowing on the Banks

Head a question angled
first to one side then the other.  A robin
listening for life under wave petunias
after a thin rain.  Lowing
sows cross rust-tinted Juniata as
river musk like cat piss fogs up hollow—
Someone must hear it as I tuck
my fiddle under chin, slide the bow
across the string:  high D
playing the spine tremolo.

**Footnote to My Living Will**

I want that burnt hue
of copper fanned out, vertical
beams of light to catch the red
under a hawk's wing.  On planes
I'm aware we're meant for rising
like this, even without slight
hollow bones, falling where faces
live abstract outlines.
The sky is not necessarily a story
our spirits can lay claim to.  Nevertheless,
burn my body when all is said and done.
If gravity can't hold me
heaven has no choice but to take.

**Amanda Passmore-Ott** teaches writing at The Pennsylvania State University for the past 17 years and lives in Hollidaysburg, Pennsylvania with her husband, three cats, and Siberian Husky. She has taught courses in creative writing as well as literature, rhetoric and composition, writing within the social sciences, ethnography, and article writing. Her poems can be found in such journals as *Tiny Seed Literary Journal, Blueline: A literary Magazine Dedicated to the Spirit of the Adirondacks, Albatross, Wavelength, and Calliope: A Journal of Women's Literature and Art.* Amanda's work often speaks to the juxtaposition of the human condition and an indifferent natural world which she experiences through hiking and traveling. In addition to teaching and writing, Amanda also plays violin in the Celtic rock band, Full Kilt, which has also taken her abroad to Ireland several times. When not in the classroom or at the writing desk, she often can be found hiking with her Siberian Husky, Onoko. The mountains speak to her and, whenever possible, she answers.